P9-EDD-668

Comparing
Countries

Compara
países

School
Life

La vida
escolar

translated into Spanish by María P Coira

Sabrina Crewe

CRABTREE
PUBLISHING COMPANY
WWW.CRABTREEBOOKS.COM

CRABTREE
PUBLISHING COMPANY
WWW.CRABTREEBOOKS.COM

Author: Sabrina Crewe

Editorial director: Kathy Middleton

Designer: Keith Williams

Illustrator: Stefan Chabluk

Translator: Maria P. Coira

Proofreader: Melissa Boyce

Production coordinator and prepress: Ken Wright

Print coordinator: Katherine Berti

Every attempt has been made to clear copyright. Should there be any inadvertent omission please apply to the publisher for rectification.

The publisher would like to thank the following for permission to reproduce their pictures: The Age/Getty Images 25; Rainier Martin Ampongan/Shutterstock 20; Anirut Thailand/Shutterstock 24; Asahi Shimbun/Getty Images 9; City Montessori School 4; Jonas Gratzer/Getty Images 28; Abd. Halim Hadi/Shutterstock 19; Wang He/Getty Images 22; Hemis/Alamy Stock Photo 27; Anton Ivanov/Shutterstock 10; Christopher Jones/Alamy Stock Photo 14; Ton Koene/Alamy Stock Photo front cover (bottom); Angela Louwe/Shutterstock front cover (top), title page, 11; Jake Lyell/Alamy Stock Photo 16; Per-Anders Pettersson/Getty Images 23; Sami Sarkis/Getty Images 26; Science Photo/Shutterstock 18; Tolga Sezgin/Shutterstock 17; Janek Skarzynski/ Getty Images 6; Kumar Sriskandan/Alamy Stock Photo 12; Kim Wendt/Rosan Bosch Studio 29; Holly Wilmeth/Getty Images 7; Brent Winebrenner/Getty Images 13; Dale Wittner/Alamy Stock Photo 5; Zero Creatives/Getty Images 21; Zzvet/Shutterstock 15.

Library and Archives Canada Cataloguing in Publication

Title: School life = La vida escolar / Sabrina Crewe.
Other titles: Vida escolar
Names: Crewe, Sabrina, author. | Coira, María P., translator.
Description: Series statement: Comparing countries = Compara países | Translated into Spanish by María P. Coira. | Previously published: London: Franklin Watts, 2018. | Includes index. | Text in English and Spanish.
Identifiers: Canadiana (print) 20190199229 | Canadiana (ebook) 20190199237 | ISBN 9780778769439 (hardcover) | ISBN 9780778769866 (softcover) | ISBN 9781427124432 (HTML)
Subjects: LCSH: Schools—Juvenile literature. | LCSH: Education—Juvenile literature.
Classification: LCC LB1556 .C74 2020 | DDC j371—dc23

Library of Congress Cataloging-in-Publication Data

Names: Crewe, Sabrina, author. | Crewe, Sabrina. School life. | Crewe, Sabrina. School life. Spanish. | Chabluk, Stefan, illustrator.
Title: School life = La vida escolar / Sabrina Crewe ; illustrator, Stefan Chabluk.
Other titles: Vida escolar
Description: New York, New York : Crabtree Publishing Company, 2020. | Series: Comparing countries | Includes index.
Identifiers: LCCN 2019043593 (print) | LCCN 2019043594 (ebook) | ISBN 9780778769439 (hardcover) | ISBN 9780778769866 (paperback) | ISBN 9781427124432 (ebook)
Subjects: LCSH: Schools--Juvenile literature.
Classification: LCC LB1556 .C74 2020 (print) | LCC LB1556 (ebook) | DDC 371--dc23
LC record available at https://lccn.loc.gov/2019043593
LC ebook record available at https://lccn.loc.gov/2019043594

Crabtree Publishing Company
www.crabtreebooks.com   1-800-387-7650

Published in 2020 by Crabtree Publishing Company

Published in Canada
Crabtree Publishing
616 Welland Avenue
St. Catharines, ON
L2M 5V6

Published in the United States
Crabtree Publishing
PMB 59051
350 Fifth Ave, 59th Floor
New York, NY 10118

Printed in the U.S.A./012020/CG20191115

First published in Great Britain in 2018 by The Watts Publishing Group
Copyright © The Watts Publishing Group 2018

Contents

To read this book in English, follow the blue boxes. To read this book in Spanish, follow the yellow boxes. Look for the globe on each page. It shows you where each country is in the world and on which continent.

Contenido

Para leer este libro en inglés, sigue los recuadros en azul. Para leer este libro en español, sigue los recuadros en amarillo. Busca el globo terráqueo en cada página. Te muestra dónde está ubicado cada país en el mundo y en qué continente.

Schools around the world

There are schools in every country. Let's go around the world to look at some of them! You can compare school life in other countries with your own.

INDIA

Schools come in different sizes. The world's biggest school is in Lucknow, India. It has more than 50,000 students and 2,500 teachers!

Escuelas alrededor del mundo

Hay escuelas en todos los países. ¡Vamos a recorrer el mundo para observar algunas de ellas! Puedes comparar la vida escolar de otros países con la tuya.

INDIA

Las escuelas son de diversos tamaños. La escuela más grande del mundo está en Lucknow, en la India. ¡Tiene más de 50,000 estudiantes y 2,500 maestros!

UNITED STATES

In the United States, some schools in the countryside have a small number of students. These small schools have just one classroom for students of all ages.

ESTADOS UNIDOS

En los Estados Unidos, algunas escuelas del campo tienen muy pocos estudiantes. Estas pequeñas escuelas tienen solo un salón de clases, para estudiantes de todas las edades.

UNITED STATES
ESTADOS UNIDOS

Europe/ Europa

Asia/Asia

Africa/ África

Australia/ Oceanía

North America/ América del Norte

Europe/ Europa

Africa/ África

South America/ América del Sur

INDIA

INDIA

5

Getting to school

Today, all over the world, children are going to and from school. They walk, cycle, or go by car. Some children go by boat, and many travel on buses.

POLAND

In Poland, the school buses are orange. The buses pick up children near their homes and bring them back again after school.

La ida a la escuela

Hoy, en todo el mundo, los niños van y vienen de la escuela. Van a pie, en bicicleta o en carro. Algunos niños van en barco, y muchos viajan en autobús.

POLONIA

En Polonia, los autobuses escolares son anaranjados. Los autobuses recogen a los niños cerca de sus casas y los traen otra vez después de la escuela.

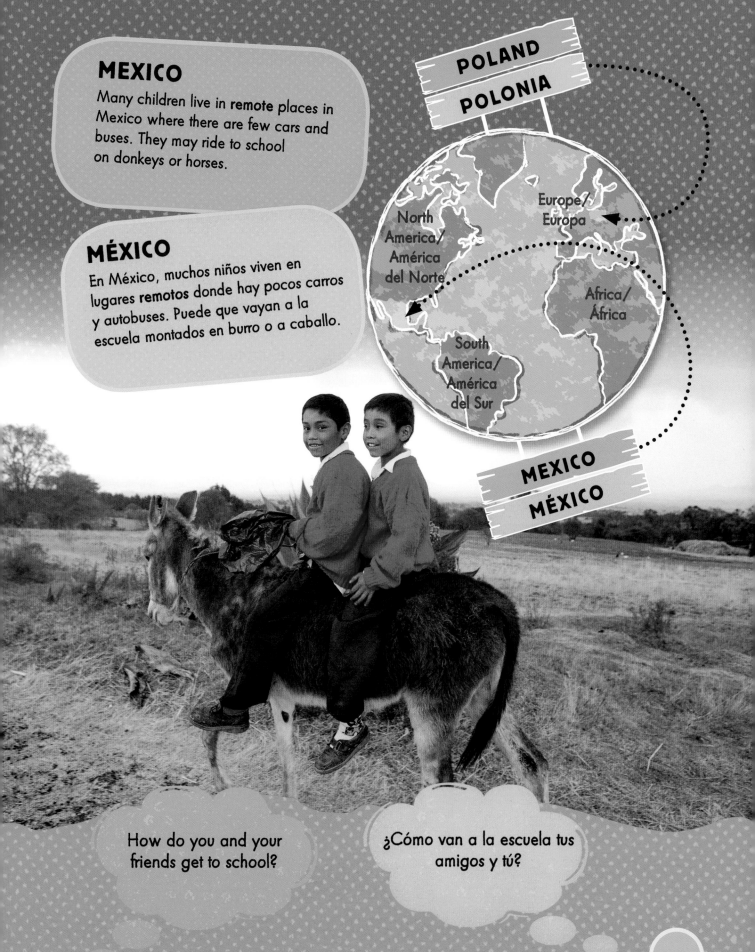

MEXICO

Many children live in **remote** places in Mexico where there are few cars and buses. They may ride to school on donkeys or horses.

MÉXICO

En México, muchos niños viven en lugares **remotos** donde hay pocos carros y autobuses. Puede que vayan a la escuela montados en burro o a caballo.

POLAND
POLONIA

North America/ América del Norte

Europe/ Europa

África/ África

South America/ América del Sur

MEXICO
MÉXICO

How do you and your friends get to school?

¿Cómo van a la escuela tus amigos y tú?

Back to school

The start of the school year is a big day for children everywhere. Some schools have special events on the first day of school.

RUSSIA

On September 1, Russians **celebrate** the first day of school as Knowledge Day. New students receive balloons and bring flowers for their teachers.

La vuelta a la escuela

El comienzo del año escolar es un gran día para los niños en todas partes. Algunas escuelas tienen actividades especiales el primer día de clases.

RUSIA

El 1.º de septiembre los rusos **celebran** el primer día de clases como el Día del Saber. Los estudiantes nuevos reciben globos y traen flores para sus maestros.

JAPAN

The new school year begins in April in Japan. On the first day, students are welcomed with an entrance **ceremony**. Some children wear **traditional** clothes.

JAPÓN

En Japón, el nuevo año escolar empieza en abril. El primer día, los estudiantes son bienvenidos con una **ceremonia** de ingreso. Algunos niños se ponen trajes **tradicionales**.

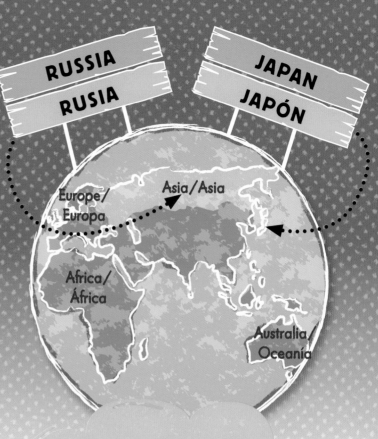

RUSSIA
RUSIA

JAPAN
JAPÓN

Europe/
Europa

Asia/Asia

Africa/
África

Australia/
Oceanía

What is a ceremony?

A ceremony is an event that marks a special occasion. Ceremonies often have speeches, songs, and awards.

¿Qué es una ceremonia?

Una ceremonia es un evento que señala una ocasión especial. En las ceremonias a menudo hay discursos, canciones y premios.

9

Uniform

In some schools, children wear their own clothes to school. In others, they have to wear a uniform.

GHANA

In Ghana, all students wear a school uniform. The pattern and color of the fabric show which school they belong to.

What is a uniform?

A uniform is a set of clothing that all members wear to show they belong to the same group. Schools and sports teams are groups that often have uniforms.

El uniforme

En algunas escuelas los niños visten su propia ropa para ir a clases. En otras tienen que vestir uniforme.

GHANA

En Ghana, todos los estudiantes visten uniforme escolar. El diseño y el color de la tela muestran a qué escuela pertenecen.

¿Qué es el uniforme?

Un uniforme es un conjunto de ropa que visten todos los miembros de un grupo para demostrar que pertenecen al mismo grupo. Las escuelas y los equipos deportivos son grupos que a menudo tienen uniformes.

INDONESIA

Many Muslim girls and women wear a headscarf. In Indonesia, the headscarf is part of the girls' school uniform.

INDONESIA

Muchas niñas y mujeres musulmanas usan un velo. En Indonesia, el velo forma parte del uniforme escolar de las niñas.

INDONESIA
INDONESIA

Europe/
Europa

Asia/Asia

Africa/
África

Australia/
Oceanía

GHANA
GHANA

11

The school day

La jornada escolar

The school day is different around the world. It is longer in some places and shorter in others.

La jornada escolar es diferente en todo el mundo. Es más larga en algunos lugares y más corta en otros.

SPAIN

Schools in Spain have a 2–3 hour break in the middle of the day. Students often go home for lunch and a rest.

ESPAÑA

Las escuelas españolas tienen un descanso de 2 a 3 horas a mitad del día. Los estudiantes a menudo van a casa a almorzar y descansar.

Too many students

Schools in some countries have a lot of students and not enough schools. In Poland, half the children go to school in the morning and the other half go in the afternoon!

Demasiados estudiantes

Las escuelas de algunos países tienen muchos estudiantes y no hay suficientes escuelas. En Polonia, ¡la mitad de los niños van por la mañana y la otra mitad van por la tarde!

SOUTH KOREA

All children in South Korea go to school during the day, but some also go to another school in the evening. Older students may study for 15 hours a day!

COREA DEL SUR

Todos los niños de Corea del Sur van a la escuela durante el día, pero algunos también van por la noche. ¡Los estudiantes mayores pueden estudiar hasta 15 horas al día!

SOUTH KOREA
COREA DEL SUR

Europe/
Europa

Asia/Asia

África/
África

Australia/
Oceanía

SPAIN
ESPAÑA

Places to learn

You may think of a classroom as a room with walls and desks. But there are other places where children can learn too.

GREAT BRITAIN

Some of the best places to learn are outside. Some schools in Great Britain hold classes outdoors to study water, plants, and animals.

Lugares para aprender

Quizá pienses en un salón de clases como un cuarto con paredes y escritorios. Pero hay otros lugares donde los niños también pueden aprender.

GRAN BRETAÑA

Algunos de los mejores lugares para aprender están afuera. Algunas escuelas de Gran Bretaña tienen clases al aire libre para estudiar el agua, las plantas y los animales.

GREAT BRITAIN
GRAN BRETAÑA

Europe/
Europa

Asia/Asia

África/
África

Australia/
Oceanía

MYANMAR
MYANMAR

MYANMAR

For part of their school life, many boys in Myanmar become Buddhist monks. Their classroom is the Buddhist monastery.

MYANMAR

Durante parte de su vida escolar, muchos niños de Myanmar se hacen monjes budistas. Su salón de clases es el monasterio budista.

School equipment

Some schools around the world have a lot of modern equipment. In other schools, students have little equipment to help them.

TANZANIA

Many schools in Tanzania have classrooms and libraries with computers. Students learn computer skills and can take part in lessons online.

Materiales escolares

Algunas escuelas del mundo tienen muchos materiales modernos. En otras escuelas, los estudiantes tienen pocos materiales de ayuda.

TANZANIA

Muchas escuela de Tanzania tienen salones y bibliotecas con computadoras. Los estudiantes aprenden computación y pueden participar en clase por Internet.

TURKEY

A lot of children have come from Syria to Turkey with their families as **refugees**. The schools for refugee children often have few supplies except pencils and paper.

TURQUÍA

Muchos niños han llegado con sus familias de Siria a Turquía como **refugiados**. Las escuelas para niños refugiados tienen pocos materiales excepto lápices y papel.

TURKEY

TURQUÍA

Europe/ Europa

Asia/Asia

África/ África

Australia/ Oceanía

TANZANIA

TANZANIA

What equipment in your school helps you the most?

¿Qué materiales de tu escuela te ayudan más?

Lessons

Las clases

Schools around the world teach reading, writing, **languages**, and math. In different parts of the world, children may have other kinds of lessons too.

Las escuelas de todo el mundo enseñan lectura, escritura, **idiomas** y matemáticas. En distintas partes del mundo, los niños pueden tener también otros tipos de clases.

GERMANY

In schools in Germany, science lessons are important. Students learn about robots, computers and other technology in labs and workshops.

ALEMANIA

En las escuelas de Alemania, las clases de ciencias son importantes. Los estudiantes aprenden sobre robots, computadoras, y otras tecnologías en laboratorios y talleres.

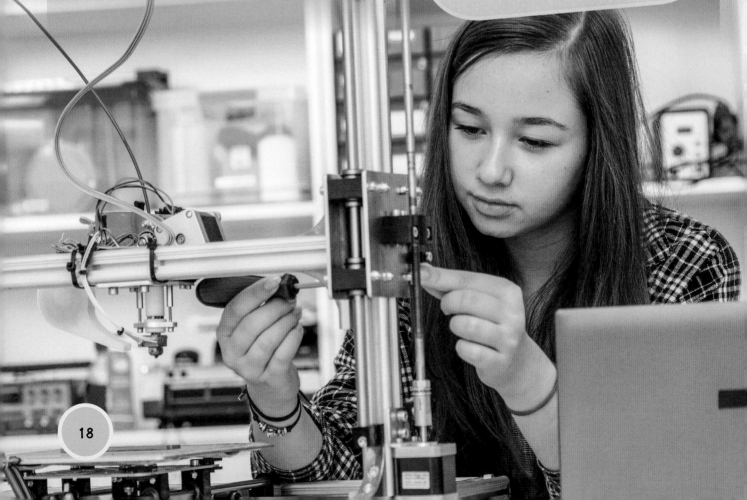

GERMANY
ALEMANIA

Europe/
Europa

Asia/Asia

África/
África

Australia/
Oceanía

SAUDI ARABIA
ARABIA SAUDITA

SAUDI ARABIA

Learning about **religion** is important in schools in Saudi Arabia. Many **mosques** have their own schools.

ARABIA SAUDITA

Aprender **religión** es importante en las escuelas de Arabia Saudita. Muchas **mezquitas** tienen su propia escuela.

Exercise!

Physical **education**, or PE for short, means it's time to exercise! In most countries, schools use PE to teach new sports and skills.

PHILIPPINES

In the Philippines, children have PE lessons every week. They do fun exercises to be active and stay healthy.

¡Ejercicio!

¡Hacer **educación física** significa que es hora de hacer ejercicio! En algunos países, las escuelas usan la clase de educación física para enseñar nuevos deportes y destrezas.

FILIPINAS

En las Filipinas, los niños tienen clase de educación física todas las semanas. Hacen ejercicios divertidos para estar activos y sanos.

What is education?

Education means gaining skills and knowledge. Part of education is learning facts and another part is learning how to do something new, like swim or speak a new language.

¿Qué es la educación?

La educación significa adquirir destrezas y conocimientos. Parte de la educación es aprender información, y otra parte es aprender a hacer algo nuevo, como nadar o hablar otro idioma.

PHILIPPINES

FILIPINAS

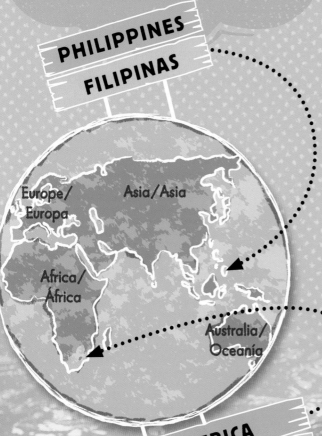

Europe/
Europa

Asia/Asia

África/
África

Australia/
Oceanía

SOUTH AFRICA

Many students in South Africa have swimming lessons in PE. Children learn different swimming strokes and take part in competitions.

SUDÁFRICA

Muchas escuelas de Sudáfrica tienen clases de natación en educación física. Los niños aprenden distintos estilos de natación y participan en competencias.

SOUTH AFRICA

SUDÁFRICA

Lunchtime

In the middle of the day, most schools stop lessons so everyone can have something to eat. Children around the world eat different things for lunch.

CHINA

In China, children eat traditional food for lunch, such as fish and vegetables. Their school lunch almost always includes rice or noodles.

La hora de almorzar

A mitad del día, la mayoría de las escuelas paran las clases para que todo el mundo pueda comer algo. En distintas partes del mundo los niños comen cosas diferentes en el almuerzo.

CHINA

En China, los niños comen alimentos tradicionales, como pescado y verduras. La comida de la escuela casi siempre incluye arroz o fideos.

22

LESOTHO

School lunch in Lesotho includes stew and pap, which is porridge made from ground maize. The cooks make lunch outside in big pots over open fires.

LESOTO

La comida escolar en Lesoto incluye guiso y pap, que es una crema hecha de maíz molido. Las cocineras preparan el almuerzo afuera, en grandes ollas sobre hogueras.

Do you eat any of the same things as these students for lunch? How is your lunch different?

¿Comes en el almuerzo algunas de estas mismas cosas? ¿En qué se diferencia tu almuerzo?

CHINA

CHINA

Europe/ Europa

Asia/Asia

Africa/ África

Australia/ Oceanía

LESOTHO

LESOTO

Fun at school

Diversión en la escuela

There are a lot of different ways to have fun during the school day.

Hay muchas maneras diferentes de divertirse durante la jornada escolar.

THAILAND

Playing in a school band is always enjoyable. In Thailand, children use traditional instruments that have been played for hundreds of years.

TAILANDIA

Tocar en una banda escolar siempre es divertido. En Tailandia, los niños usan instrumentos tradicionales que se han tocado durante cientos de años.

What is your favorite way to have fun at school?

¿Cuál es tu manera favorita de divertirte en la escuela?

NEW ZEALAND

Making things at school is a fun way to learn. Many schools in New Zealand teach children about healthy foods through cooking lessons.

NUEVA ZELANDA

Hacer cosas en la escuela es una manera divertida de aprender. En muchas escuelas de Nueva Zelanda se enseña acerca de los alimentos saludables mediante clases de cocina.

Asia/Asia

North America/ América del Norte

South America/ América del Sur

Australia/ Oceanía

Europe/ Europa

Asia/Asia

Africa/ África

Australia/ Oceanía

NEW ZEALAND
NUEVA ZELANDA

THAILAND
TAILANDIA

Learning at home

Aprender en casa

After school, some children have homework to do. Other children do all their learning at home.

Después de la escuela, algunos niños tienen que hacer la tarea. Otros niños hacen todo su aprendizaje en casa.

FRANCE

At 4:30 p.m., most children in France go home to eat with their families and do their homework. It is usual for older children to have two hours of homework to do.

FRANCIA

A las 4.30 de la tarde, la mayoría de los niños en Francia van a casa para comer con sus familias y hacer la tarea. Es normal que los niños mayores franceses tengan que hacer dos horas de tarea.

AUSTRALIA

AUSTRALIA

FRANCE

FRANCIA

Europe/
Europa

Asia/Asia

Africa/
África

Australia/
Oceanía

AUSTRALIA

In Australia, some children live so far away from schools that they have to learn at home. They **communicate** with teachers using the Internet or special radios that send and receive messages.

AUSTRALIA

En Australia, algunos niños viven tan lejos de las escuelas que tienen que aprender en casa. Se **comunican** con los maestros usando Internet o unas radios especiales que envían y reciben mensajes.

Amazing schools

Some schools are in unusual places, and others may have unusual ways of teaching. They may not even look like schools at all!

Escuelas increíbles

Algunas escuelas están en lugares poco comunes, y otras pueden tener maneras poco comunes de enseñar. ¡Puede que no parezcan escuelas en absoluto!

BANGLADESH

The floating schools of Bangladesh are boats that bring education to children cut off by floods. The school boats travel along rivers to visit and teach students in different villages.

BANGLADESH

Las escuelas flotantes de Bangladesh son barcos que llevan la educación a niños aislados por inundaciones. Los barcos-escuela viajan por los ríos para visitar y enseñar a los estudiantes de distintos pueblos.

SWEDEN

Vittra schools are free schools in Sweden with open spaces instead of classrooms with walls. Children can choose what to learn and where to study.

SUECIA

Las escuelas Vittra son escuelas gratuitas de Suecia que tienen espacios abiertos en vez de salones con paredes. Los niños pueden elegir qué aprender y dónde estudiar.

BANGLADESH

BANGLADESH

Europe/
Europa

Asia/Asia

África/
África

Australia/
Oceanía

SWEDEN

SUECIA

29

Glossary

celebrate To do something special for a happy or important event; for example, having a party for someone's birthday

ceremony An event that marks a special occasion, such as a wedding or award-giving. Ceremonies often have speeches, songs, or awards.

communicate To exchange information by speaking or writing or in other ways

education Skills and knowledge gained through learning

equipment Supplies, tools, or anything needed to perform a task

flood An area of water on land that is usually dry; for example, when lots of rain causes a river to overflow its banks

headscarf A piece of cloth that goes over a person's head

language The words a group of people understand and use to communicate with each other. Countries have their own languages, but so do smaller groups within countries, such as tribes.

maize A type of grain, also known as corn, that is grown for food

modern Most recent

monastery The place where a group of monks live together and work or study

monk A man who leaves the everyday world to live in a religious community and devote himself to religion

mosque A place of worship, community, culture, and learning for Muslims

refugee A person who leaves their homeland because of war or other danger and seeks shelter and safety in another place or country

religion A set of spiritual beliefs shared by a group of people, such as Buddhists, Christians, Hindus, or Muslims. Many religions also worship gods and offer people rules and values to live by.

remote Far away from a town or city

technology Scientific knowledge, processes, or tools that people can use to do things; for example, the use of computers for work or learning

traditional Always done in the same way and passed on to younger people in a family or community

uniform A set of clothing that all members wear to show they belong to the same group

Glosario

(celebrate) celebrar Hacer algo especial para señalar un acontecimiento alegre o importante; por ejemplo, hacer una fiesta en el cumpleaños de alguien

(ceremony) ceremonia Acto que señala una ocasión especial, como una boda o una entrega de premios. En las ceremonias a menudo hay discursos, canciones o premios.

(communicate) comunicar Intercambiar información hablando o escribiendo o de otras maneras

(education) educación Destrezas y conocimientos adquiridos mediante el aprendizaje

(equipment) materiales Artículos, instrumentos o cualquier cosa necesaria para realizar un trabajo

(flood) inundación Masa de agua sobre tierra que normalmente es seca; por ejemplo, cuando grandes lluvias hacen que un río se desborde

(headscarf) velo Trozo de tela que va sobre la cabeza de una persona

(language) idioma Palabras que un grupo de personas entiende y usa para comunicarse entre sí. Los países tienen sus propios idiomas, pero también los tienen grupos más pequeños dentro de un país, como las tribus.

(maize) maíz Tipo de grano cultivado como alimento

(modern) moderno Muy reciente

(monastery) monasterio Lugar donde en grupo de monjes viven juntos, trabajan y estudian

(monk) monje Hombre que deja el mundo cotidiano para vivir en una comunidad religiosa y dedicarse a la religión

(mosque) mezquita Lugar de oración, comunidad, cultura y aprendizaje de los musulmanes

(refugee) refugiado Persona que deja su tierra natal debido a una guerra o a otro peligro y busca refugio y seguridad en otro lugar o país

(religion) religión Conjunto de creencias espirituales que comparten un grupo de personas, como los budistas, cristianos, hindúes o musulmanes. Muchas religiones también adoran dioses y ofrecen a las personas reglas y valores para que vivan de acuerdo a ellos.

(remote) remoto Lejos de un pueblo o ciudad

(technology) tecnología Conocimientos, procesos o instrumentos científicos que se pueden usar para hacer cosas; por ejemplo, usar computadoras para trabajar o aprender

(traditional) tradicional Siempre hecho de la misma manera y que pasa a los miembros más jóvenes de una familia o comunidad

(uniform) uniforme Conjunto de ropa que visten todos los miembros de un grupo para demostrar que pertenecen al mismo grupo

Index

Índice

El índice español no sigue el mismo orden que el inglés.